The Harbour

Meredith Hooper
Illustrated by Peter Kent

Scarborough Harbour

CAMBRIDGE UNIVERSITY PRESS

A long time ago, the Romans came here.

There was a safe harbour for their ships.

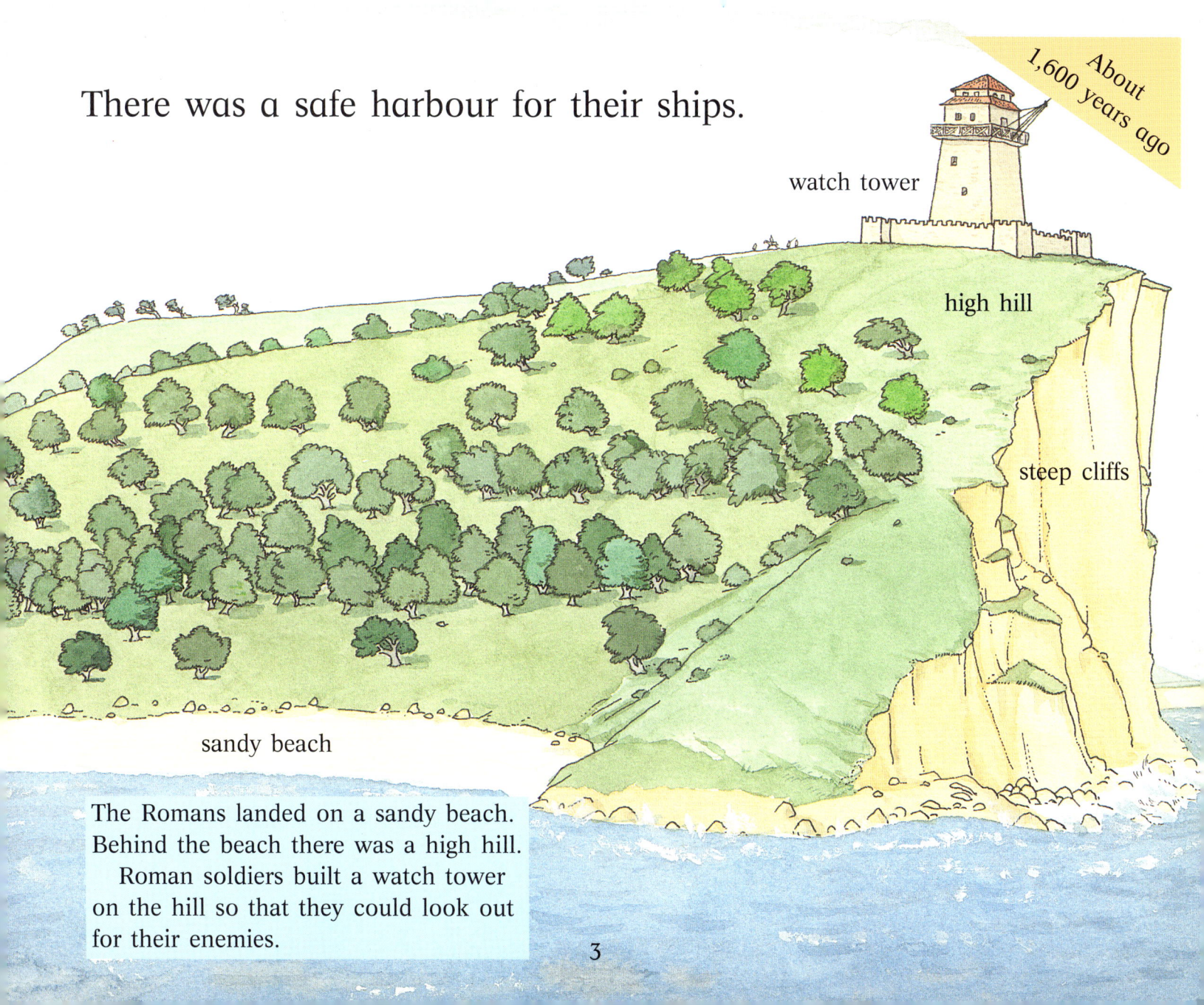

About 1,600 years ago

watch tower

high hill

steep cliffs

sandy beach

The Romans landed on a sandy beach. Behind the beach there was a high hill. Roman soldiers built a watch tower on the hill so that they could look out for their enemies.

Many years later, Vikings came in their longboats.

They liked the harbour, so they built their houses here, next to the beach.

About 1,000 years ago

The Vikings decided to stay here because there was a safe harbour for their ships and there were plenty of fish for them to catch in the sea.

Ships began to come to the harbour from many countries.

The ships brought lots of things to sell in the busy town.

About 700 years ago

People from the town built a wide stone wall at the edge of the harbour. Now sailors could unload everything from the ships onto the wall.

Sailors carried barrels of wine and baskets of fish off the ships.

Workmen unloaded building stones for the castle, which stood on the hill, high above the harbour.

Many people from the town worked at the harbour.

rope walk

sail-loft

Shipbuilders worked at the shipyards. The ships were built from oak trees cut down in nearby forests.
   Ropemakers made ropes in long buildings near the castle. Nails and wire were made in workshops at the harbour. Sails were made in special high buildings called sail-lofts.

Boys and men from the town went to sea.
They worked as sailors and fishermen.

About 300 years ago

Every year, bad storms sent waves crashing into the harbour. Sometimes ships were wrecked.

The people in the town built a strong new wall to make the harbour safer for ships.

About 200 years ago

Workmen dropped heavy rocks into the sea. Then they built a wide, strong wall on top of the rocks.

The waves crashed against the outside of the wall. Ships could shelter from the storms inside the wall, which was like a safe arm around the harbour.

More and more ships came to the harbour.
The town became bigger and busier.

A light flashed on top of a lighthouse to show the sailors the way to the harbour.

About 100 years ago

New steamships, tall sailing-ships and busy fishing boats all used the harbour. Cranes unloaded the ships' cargoes.

Now, many ships are too big to come into the harbour. Small ships and fishing boats can still use the harbour.

Many people visit the harbour at Scarborough.
They like to look at the lighthouse and the boats.

Today

People like to visit the castle and to stand on the hill where the Roman soldiers once stood.

Index

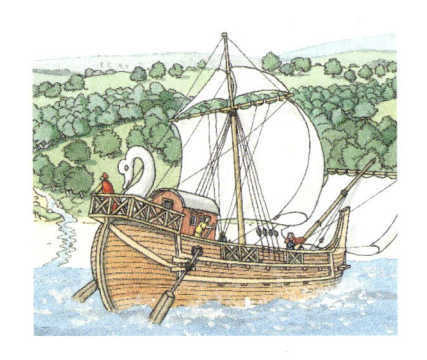

beach pages 3, 5

castle pages 7, 8, 15

fishing boats pages 13, 14

hill pages 3, 7, 15

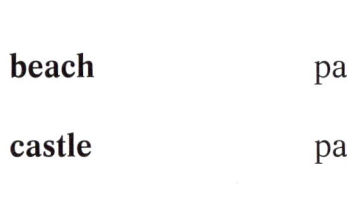

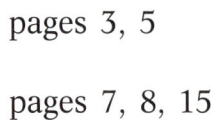

lighthouse pages 13, 15

Romans pages 2–3, 15

sailors pages 7, 9, 13

shipyards page 8

storms page 10

Vikings pages 4–5

wall pages 7, 11

watch tower page 3